READING POWER

Technology That Changed the World

The Radio
The World Tunes In

Joanne Mattern

The Rosen Publishing Group's
PowerKids Press™
New York

Published in 2003 by The Rosen Publishing Group, Inc.
29 East 21st Street, New York, NY 10010

First Edition

Book Design: Michael DeLisio

Photo Credits: Cover © Digital Stock; pp. 4, 5 © Photodisc; pp. 6, 7, 8, 12, 13, 14, 15 Culver Pictures; pp. 9, 11 Michael DeLisio; p. 10 © IndexStock; p. 11 © Corbis; p. 12 National Archives, Still Picture Branch; p. 17 © AP/Wide World Photos; p. 18 © Bettmann/Corbis; p. 19 © Corbis; p. 21 © Adrian Arbib/Corbis

Library of Congress Cataloging-in-Publication Data

Mattern, Joanne, 1963-
The radio : the world tunes in / Joanne Mattern.
    p. cm. — (Technology that changed the world)
Summary: Presents information on radio, including its invention, history, how it works, and how it has affected people's lives.
Includes bibliographical references and index.
ISBN 0-8239-6491-4 (library binding)
1. Radio—Juvenile literature. [1. Radio.] I. Title.
TK6550.7 .M38 2003
384.5—dc21

                                                    2002000524

Contents

The Beginnings of Radio

The telegraph and the telephone were invented in the 1800s. These inventions let people send messages over many miles. The telegraph and the telephone used wires to send messages. However, scientists wanted to find a way to send messages without using wires.

The telegraph sent messages in clicks.

The telephone sent voice messages.

In 1864, James Clerk Maxwell wrote about a kind of electrical energy that he believed traveled through the air. This energy would later be called radio waves. During the 1880s, Heinrich Hertz did tests that proved Maxwell's idea was right.

James Clerk Maxwell

Heinrich Hertz

In 1895, Guglielmo Marconi *(GOOG-lee-ehl-moh mar-KOH-nee)* became the first person to send a signal through the air using radio waves. In 1901, he sent signals across the Atlantic Ocean, from England to Canada. These signals carried a message that was turned into sound when they were received in Canada.

Marconi and one of his early wire-free telegraph inventions

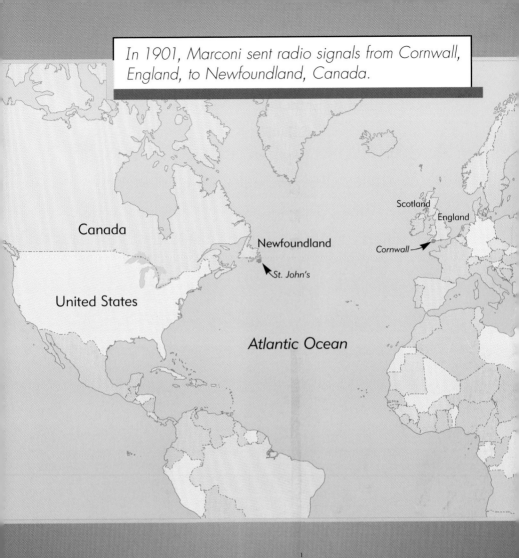

In 1901, Marconi sent radio signals from Cornwall, England, to Newfoundland, Canada.

Scotland
England
Cornwall →
Canada
Newfoundland
↖St. John's
United States
Atlantic Ocean

Now You Know

The first broadcast of a person's voice happened in 1906. Reginald Fessenden spoke by radio from Massachusetts to ships in the Atlantic Ocean.

9

How a Radio Works

A radio works by receiving signals sent by a transmitter. A transmitter changes sound, such as music or people's voices, into radio waves. Then, the transmitter sends the radio waves through the air and through space. A receiver in a radio changes the radio waves back into sounds that you can hear.

By pressing buttons or turning dials on a radio, people pick the signals of the radio station they want to hear. Picking up signals like this is called tuning in.

Radio station transmitter

A radio station uses a transmitter to broadcast, or send, radio waves to a radio. Radio waves can go through hard objects, such as walls of buildings.

11

Radio and the World

The radio changed the way people lived. People were able to learn about things going on all around the world. People listened to important news as it happened. They also listened to sports, comedies, plays, music, and children's programs.

From the 1920s to the early 1950s, many families would gather in their living rooms to listen to their favorite radio shows.

In the United States, two of the first radio stations to broadcast were KDKA in Pittsburgh, Pennsylvania, and WWJ in Detroit, Michigan. Both started in 1920.

Many movie stars, such as Cary Grant (left) and Greer Garson, could be heard on radio programs.

13

During World War II, President Franklin D. Roosevelt often spoke to the nation on the radio.

Franklin D. Roosevelt was president of the United States from 1933 to 1945. His talks on the radio helped Americans feel safer during World War II.

In 1945, newspaper workers were on strike in New York City. Mayor Fiorello La Guardia (fee-uh-REH-loh luh-GWAR-dee-uh) *read newspaper comic strips on the radio to people who could not get the newspaper.*

Now You Know

On October 30, 1938, a radio station broadcast "The War of the Worlds." It was a science fiction story about aliens from Mars landing in New Jersey. Many listeners across the country got scared. They thought the story was true. Orson Welles was the star of the show.

Orson Welles

Keeping Up with the Times

When television became popular in the 1950s, radio stations had to change to keep people listening. Stations began playing a new kind of music called rock and roll, which many young people liked to hear. Stations also broadcast talk shows and all-news shows.

Now You Know

In 1952, Americans owned about 105 million radios. At that time, about half of the cars in the United States had radios.

The people at a radio station who talk and play music during a radio program are called disc jockeys. In the 1950s, Wolfman Jack was a disc jockey who played rock-and-roll music for radio listeners.

As time passed, scientists made changes to the radio. Radios were made smaller so that people could easily take them anywhere.

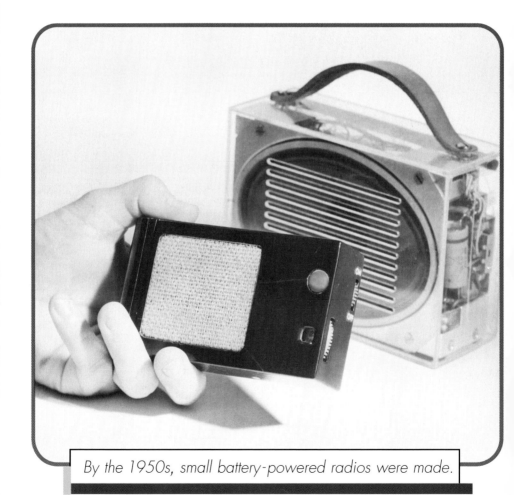

By the 1950s, small battery-powered radios were made.

People were able to use smaller radios everywhere they went.

Radio Today

Radio is as popular now as ever before. Today, there are over 10,000 radio stations in the United States. Americans own about 550 million radios. Almost every car in America has a radio.

Every country in the world has at least one radio station. The radio has changed life for people everywhere.

People around the world use the radio to get the latest news and entertainment.

Time Line

1864:	James Clerk Maxwell writes about radio waves.
1880s:	Heinrich Hertz proves Maxwell's idea about radio waves is right.
1895:	Guglielmo Marconi sends radio signals a few miles through the air.
1901:	Marconi sends radio signals across the Atlantic Ocean.
1906:	Reginald Fessenden is the first person to have his voice broadcast on the radio.
1919:	Woodrow Wilson is the first U.S. president to speak on the radio.
1925–1950:	Radio is the main source of family home entertainment.

Glossary

aliens (**ay**-lyuhnz) beings that are not from Earth

broadcast (**brawd**-kast) to send out radio or television signals; a radio or television show

electrical (ih-**lehk**-truh-kuhl) having to do with power that is used to make light, heat, or motion

energy (**ehn**-uhr-jee) power that can be used to produce heat or make machines work

inventions (ihn-**vehn**-shuhnz) new things that someone thinks of or makes

popular (**pahp**-yuh-luhr) liked by many people

program (**proh**-gram) a radio or television show

radio waves (**ray**-dee-oh **wayvz**) electrical energy that travels through the air

receiver (rih-**see**-vuhr) the part of a radio that gathers radio waves and changes them into sounds

signal (**sihg**-nuhl) an electrical wave that sends sounds and pictures to radios and televisions

transmitter (tran-**smit**-uhr) something that changes sounds into radio waves and sends them through the air

Resources

Books

Guglielmo Marconi: Radio Pioneer
by Beverly Birch
Blackbirch Press (2001)

Radio
by George Coulter and Shirley Coulter
Rourke Publications (1996)

Web Sites

Due to the changing nature of Internet links, PowerKids Press has developed an on-line list of Web sites related to the subjects of this book. This site is updated regularly. Please use this link to access the list:

http://www.powerkidslinks.com/tcw/radio/

Index

B
broadcast, 9, 11, 13, 15–16, 21

E
energy, 6

H
Hertz, Heinrich, 6–7, 21

I
inventions, 4, 8

M
Marconi, Guglielmo, 8–9, 21

Maxwell, James Clerk, 6, 21

P
program, 12–13, 17

R
radio station, 10–11, 13, 16–17, 20
radio waves, 6, 8, 10–11, 21
receiver, 10

S
signal, 8–10, 21

T
transmitter, 10–11

Word Count: 473

Note to Librarians, Teachers, and Parents

If reading is a challenge, Reading Power is a solution! Reading Power is perfect for readers who want high-interest subject matter at an accessible reading level. These fact-filled, photo-illustrated books are designed for readers who want straightforward vocabulary, engaging topics, and a manageable reading experience. With clear picture/text correspondence, leveled Reading Power books put the reader in charge. Now readers have the power to get the information they want and the skills they need in a user-friendly format.